The Circuit of Power

Wise Men,Military,Industry

An Experimental Political System

The parliament is an institution that represents the circuit of power.

A new political system exists in the minds of the thinkers.The triangle of councils of the wise,the military and the industrialists will have the control of the state and will be placed above everyone else.The parliament in this fantastic system will represent the ideas and the will of these 3 groups or social classes.

To achieve victory we have to take the military on our side.

Any organization which wants to take world power must take the guardians on its side.

The brain of the political body is placed above all.

The councils of the wise must be placed above the other two pillars of power.The experts on every issue will give advice and will guide like the brain guides the arms and the legs.The wise men are counselors.

The stabilizing factor of the military.Producing security.

The industrialists design economic policies.

The parliamentarians are agents of the triad of power.

The triad of power are owners of the state.

The worker is the lower class in the social hierarchy.

The wise men will protect the worker.

Clients exist since Ancient Rome.

The committees of the wise are placed above all.

Every social group will make sacrifices to achieve the national goal.

Social stratification will bring social progress.

What is freedom?

What is democracy if not the consensus of mediocrity?

The triad are veto players.

The role of the media in totalitarian and egalitarian regimes.

Customary law is more difficult to alter than official law.

Israel is a model state.

Assymetry of information and lack of democracy and equality in interethnic relations.

The scientific mind and subjectivity in political science

The problem of checks and balances.

Not what is right but what the public opinion will agree with,the democratic inefficiency.

What if all the regimes are created by a central authority?

The politician as a broker.

The right proportion between innovation and tradition,simple and complex.

The right proportion between meritocracy and nepotism.

The journalist as a broker.

The control the international banking system and the flow of money with the adjustment of interest rates.If you control the interest rates you control everything else,the army,the industrialists and the experts.

What is the cause of the bankruptcy of nations.

Is legalism and ethics more important than the national instinct for survival and self-perservation?

Why politics is defined by the mass ledia.

War is essential.The eternal need for coflict.

The militaristic nations have achieved great things.

The worship of money and the wealthy philosopher.

The role of the councils of the wise.

Create the laws in the basis of mathematical models.Put a grade on everyone,give them their objective value according to some principles,like beauty,strength,intelligence.The people with the highest score will direct the people with the lower score.This method will create a social hierarchy.

The Greek politician as an ascete.

The Greek philosophy of relative ethics.If you are beautiful you are walking in the right path,if you are ugly try to have a nice personality,which means that if you are beautiful you have the right to be mean.

The Greek aestheticism and the perfection of the form.The worship of beauty as the new God.

Hierarchy among nations.

The myth of equality.

The right proportion between liberty and stratification.

Doing politics according to what the media will say.

The military is more adept at politics.

The problem of controlling the controller.

Liberty, the supreme principle of the Western civilization.

The right ratio between liberty and structure.

The limit of liberty.

The role of the media after democracy.Mass democracy in the era of the media colonization in politics.

Political lobbies and their influence on economic policies.

The case of Turkey's militarism and its rise to superpower status.

Obama's strategy to create new alliances with India and China.

Power and interdependence with Russia.

Russia's strategic relation with Turkey.

Israel's strategy in the Middle East.

Peripheral cold wars and pairs of opponents.Israel versus Iran.North Korea versus South Korea.

The limits of democracy.

How modern mass democracy really works.

Bipolarity between the West and the East will produce a more stable international balance of power.

A scenario of Israel's relations with its neighbors.

A scenario of World War 3 and its purpose.

Less nuclear heads equals more wars.

If terrorists get nuclear material in their hands ,Nato countries will have the right to use nuclear weapons against them.

Why Iran will get nuclear technology.

Israel,the eternally persecuted nation.

Africa's hunger problem will be solved with genetically modified crops.

Why Argentina collapsed?

Greece is a country where we can apply the new utopian political model to test it and see how it works.

The military has an incentive to develop and industrial base.

How Greece was led to bankruptcy.

Greek power and the conflict between elite groups.

The German curse.How Germany caused the bankruptcy.

How Russia will spend its petrodollars.

The American wars in the Middle East have the purpose to secure the flow of oil to the Western markets.

The choice of isolation and introversion for America.

The future of the Greek-Turkish relationship.

How Germany influenced the Greek political decisions through German corporations.

The future of Israel's expansion.

Why Russia invests in nanotechnology. The attempt for leapfrogging.

In an ideal society the wise man has more power than the military and the industry.

System design and world peace.The Security Council.

Laws against war and the conflict with customary international law.

The adequate ratio between aggressiveness and law obedience.

What is law if not the will of the mighty?

The winner creates the law.

National aggressiveness is essential for survival.

Militarism versus corporatism and the wise expert as the adjuster or the mediator.

Venezouela and bipolarity.

The differences in the nature of races,creates different political systems.

Democratic and fascist regimes.

The duty of a minister of foreign affairs is to allways create balance of power around the world.

What will happen of China becomes a nationalistic state and decides to maximize power,by following the tactics of a superpower.

Laws of war.

Ethnic cleansing and genocide.

Islamic terrorism will never end.

The war between Israel and the Palestinians will never end.

Ancient families and global conspiracies.

Move the conflict in the area of the opponent.Russia against Georgia.

Scientific realism.Mathematics and empirical observations.

The revolution that prevails creates law.

The study of patterns of history for decision makers.

The study of the law is essential to learn the rules of the game.

The political systems make cycles.

The political parties of the future will be divided between supporters and haters of new technologies,like genetic engineering and nanotechnology.

The new presidents will be cyborgs who come from the ancient families.

Experimental states.

What is the essence of the will of the people and how it is defined.

Realism is to study the other players and be ready for the worst.Act like your enemies have an aggressive predisposition towards you.

Globalization enforces the mixing of the races.Every race is mixing but the chosen ones,keep their blood clean.Obviously they know something more than the rest who are ignorant.

The president must have the perfection of the form.

Politainment is the new way of doing politics.

They try to criminalize politics.

The privatization of the Organization of Horseracing.

How I will improve the position of the horseracing company when I take it from the government.

Entry of the organization in internet betting.

Advertisments of horseracing in television and the internet.

I will attract customers from other countries through the internet and satelite television.

Buses of the company will carry sports fans and visitors from the center of the city to the racetrack and back,for free.

I will upgrade the webpage of the organization which will be translated to foreign languages.

I will develop a marketing plan to increase the players of horsebetting.

I will decrease the administration costs.

The agents of the company will be more friendly and more open to attract new customers.

More information to the journalists to increase the involvement of the press and the media in horseracing.

Decrase the percentage of money that is returned to the players as profits.

Train the agents of betting to be frendlier.

Publish new books with information about horseraces and horsebetting.

The broad masses of people have to learn about horsebetting.

Publish a newspaper about horsebetting.

Start new negotiations for the debt with the banks ,to achieve better terms for the loans and lower interest rates.

Build a hotel next to the racetrack.

Make deals with travel offices to organize visits to the racetrack

Build a thematic park and restaurants next to the racetrack.

With my brainwaves I can connect to some higher spirits because the brain is a radio transmitter and radioreceiver.

The prophet sees that dark days are coming.

The Americans don't have to control every single country in the world.

Instead they can create relations of cooperation with those that want to cooperate with them,and let the rest cooperate with each other in different coalitions.

The realism of war in the Middle East.The right to self defence exists forstates and individuals.The Israeli army attacked foreign vessels that carried humanitarian aid to Gaza.The activists started to hit the Israeli soldiers with rods so they gave the right to them to defend themselves.

In the "dock" in Israel for the killing operation

Jump representatives of the Turkish government in Israel received corpses and wounded. Good health of the Greek mission. Confrontation in the UN Security Council for the bloodshed in international waters. Nine dead, condemned Israel, the European Union.

In Israel today traveling representatives of the Turkish government to seek the repatriation of corpses and injured as activists of the convoy were attacked by Israeli commandos, and was in international waters, carrying humanitarian assistance to Gaza.

The spokesman of the Israeli army said that they are free people who were aboard the convoy. As said, all the Greeks of the mission is in good health

Heated debate at the special meeting of the UN Security Council, designed to attack the Israeli army during the international fleet that was carrying humanitarian aid to Gaza. Earlier, the ambassadors of EU countries agreed on a "condemnatory" text against Israel and called for conducting an "independent" investigation.

Also, the ambassadors of member countries of NATO will meet Tuesday in special session at the request of Turkey. "An extraordinary meeting of the NATO Council with the participation of 28 ambassadors from member countries of NATO prepares for Tuesday afternoon at the request of Turkish authorities," it said in a statement to the Agency from its headquarters in Brussels.

Heated debate in the UN Security Council

Turkish Foreign Minister Ahmed
Davutoglu said yesterday at the opening
of the extraordinary session of the UN
Security Council that Israel has "lost all
international legitimacy." In his speech at
the opening of the extraordinary Mr.
Davutoglu said that Israel committed "a
serious crime totally ignoring all the
values we adopt in establishing the
United Nations.

"It's a huge violation of international law.
In simple terms, this compares with
piracy and crime, murder on behalf of the
state, "said Mr. Davutoglu. "A state that
follows this path has lost all legitimacy,
despite being a member of the
international community, led by the
Turkish foreign minister.

Instead, the representative of Israel to the UN accused the International flotilla to Gaza have had purposes other than humanitarian, arguing during the debate in the Security Agency for the bloody attack against the Israeli army convoy. "Although the media described as a humanitarian mission, which carried aid to Gaza, the flotilla that had nothing to do with a humanitarian mission," said the deputy ambassador to the Security of Israel to the UN, Daniel karma.

"What kind of humanitarian mission requires that bypass the UN, the Red Cross and other internationally recognized authorities?" He wondered. "What kind of humanitarian mission use knives, sticks and other weapons to attack soldiers who boarded a ship in accordance with international laws," he added. "There is no humanitarian crisis in

Gaza," said Karma, adding that the goods and materials destined for the Palestinian territories will be promoted through the authorized border crossings.

The Israeli diplomat noted that the Gaza Strip are "occupied by terrorists, who overthrew the Palestinian Authority during a violent coup" and that "the land of guns flowing constantly, even by sea.

Moreover, the Brazilian Foreign Minister Amorim Selsou asked the UN to take "action" and to adopt a "resounding statement" on the bloody intervention of the Israeli army in the international flotilla to Gaza. "There can only be aghast at such an event. I hope that the Security Council will adopt a resounding declaration. We really need a UN action, because this attack is very hard to leave scars, "said Amorim reporters in Brasilia.

He described the Israeli attack as a "very serious act" and said "we hope the UN will take measures that Israel will honor as would be required.

Condemnatory text from the EU

The ambassadors of EU countries agreed on a "condemnatory" text on Israel for violence against the freedom of boats carrying humanitarian aid in Gaza and call making "independent" research, said a diplomatic source AFP. 'The European Union condemns the violence which caused many casualties among the members of the fleet and called the investigation a prompt, full and independent of the facts and circumstances of the "highlighted in the text.

This declaration of the EU decided at an

emergency meeting of 27 EU countries is more intense than the first reaction of the head of EU diplomacy Catherine Ashton. The above statement is aimed specifically at Israeli military tactics against activists, while calling for an independent investigation carried out immediately.

The text also expressed deep regret for the loss of lives and called upon all sides to "reduce tension", and "underlined the necessity to continue the indirect negotiations" between Israel and the Palestinians.

Many MEPs were on the humanitarian convoy, which had sailed towards the secluded shores of the Gaza Strip.

Earlier, EU High Representative Catherine Ashton called Israel "a full investigation into" this raid, said representative. Catherine Ashton reiterated that the European Union "the policy of exclusion of Gaza is still unacceptable and not constructive" and called for ending the blockade and the "immediate and unconditional" opening of Gaza crossing to humanitarian aid, commercial goods and people.

Spain, which holds the presidency of the European Union today called the Israeli ambassador in Madrid for an explanation. For its part, the Belgian Cooperation Minister Louis Michel denounced the use of disproportionate force by the Israeli army.

Several MEPs were on the convoy which brought hundreds of activists and humanitarian aid for residents of Gaza.

Nine dead

A total of nine activists are dead after attacked by Israeli commandos in a ship belonging to an international flotilla of humanitarian aid to Gaza, the Israeli army said. A spokeswoman for the Israeli forces said that the press reflects the final number of dead after the arrival of the ship in the Israeli port Ashdod.

The Army stresses that the violence erupted when activists attacked the marines, injuring seven of them and removing guns from the other two. Israeli authorities maintain that about 20 activists were injured. The army did not disclose the nationality of any of the victims, but a senior government said that most Turks were killed.

Complete explanations requested by Ban

Ki-moon

The UN Secretary General Ban Ki-moon said shocked by the severity of the incident to humanitarian convoy, condemned the death of activists and said that it is extremely important to conduct a full investigation.

'It is vital to conduct a full investigation into the exact circumstances of the bloodshed. I believe that Israel must urgently give a full explanation, "said UN Secretary General.

Moreover, the UN High Commissioner for Human Rights Navi Pilate said "shocked" by the storming of the Israeli army. The Pilate condemned Israel's policy of imposing strict sanctions on Gaza, saying that "the exclusion continues to affect human rights on a daily basis. This situation deprives what the people need to live a normal and dignified life. Condemn once again the discriminatory shooting rockets from Gaza on Israeli territory. "

Moreover, Mr. Richard Falcone, the UN special rapporteur for the Palestinian territories, today called on the international community to bring to justice "the murderers of unarmed civilians. The official explained that the call for "both the political leadership of Israel, who gave the orders for the firm, and military leadership, who implemented the operation.

"Israel is the culprit for the use of lethal weapons against unarmed civilians," said Mr. Falcone, "civilians were in international waters and therefore enjoyed the right of unrestricted movement. Israeli naval blockade of the coastal Gaza Strip, Mr. Falcone called "crime against humanity." He asked, "as a moral and political imperative" tough sanctions against Israel by the international community.

U.S.: Understanding the conditions

The U.S. expressed its deep regret at the deaths and injuries: "The U.S. deep regret for the loss of lives and caused injuries and is currently working to understand circumstances surrounding this tragedy," noted spokesman White House William Burton of Chicago, where is the American President Barack Obama.

Moreover, the U.S. president Barack Obama has expressed the Israeli Prime Minister Netanyahu today Beniamin very sorry for the loss of lives. Also encouraged to collect all information about what happened as soon as possible, announced by the White House.

Mr. Obama on the phone with Mr. Netanyahu also said that he understood his decision to cancel the scheduled Tuesday visit to the White House and return to Israel. Both sides agreed that there would be "the first opportunity for" a meeting.

"The President expressed his deep regret at the loss of life in today's bloody attack, while it expressed concern about the fate of the wounded. Additionally, the president said the great importance of fully informed of all events and the precise circumstances of the present tragedy as soon as possible, "added the White House.

It is noteworthy that Israeli Defense Minister Ehud Barak telephoned U.S. Secretary of Hillary Clinton and National Security Adviser James Jones U.S. to give information about the attack on the international fleet for Gaza.

The Barak argued that the interference was the convoy of six ships, which took place in international waters, was in line with international maritime law and described the events before the conflict on the Turkish vessel mauve Marmara: The Marmara passengers attacked the soldiers with whatever purpose they had in their possession and wounded some. The soldiers defended themselves, "says the communiqué.

Protests in many countries

Several thousand people demonstrated

yesterday in Sweden, Denmark and Norway, to denounce the bloody Israeli commando attack on a convoy of international humanitarian assistance to Gaza.

In Sweden, about 6,000 people took to the streets of Copenhagen shouting "Boycott Israel", or "Israel in The Hague, where is the International Criminal Court and waving Palestinian flags and signs with slogans such as" there will be other ships to Gaza.

Several demonstrations were relevant to other cities in Sweden, with several thousand people in Gothenburg and 600 in Malmö.

In Denmark, hundreds of people gathered outside the Israeli embassy, on the outskirts of Copenhagen, with slogans like

"End the massacre of civilians" and "Freedom to Palestine". "I do not understand why Lego games, or incubators, for children who suffer from exclusion, may pose a threat to Israel's security," said Dr. Kamal Kouresi, spokesman for the opposition Socialist People's Party.

Norway, several hundred protesters gathered outside the Israeli embassy in Oslo, where they burned and some Israeli flags.

Shocked says Blair

Thrilled spokesman Quartet on the Middle East Tony Blair to the Israeli offensive. "I express my deep regret and I shocked at this terrible loss of life," said Blair in a statement. 'Obviously there must be a full investigation of what happened, "he adds.

www.ingramcontent.com/pod-product-compliance
Lightning Source LLC
Chambersburg PA
CBHW071257280526
45788CB00004B/1738